101 Frank Sinatra Hits for Buskers

0892205656.

Barbara.

H662200

Manor Glen

Tullogh,

GW00419125

Exclusive Distributors:
Music Sales Limited, 8/9 Frith Street, London W1V 5TZ, England.
Music Sales Pty Limited, 120 Rothschild Avenue, Rosebery, NSW 2018, Australia.

Order No. AM936419
ISBN 0-7119-5854-8
This book © Copyright 1996 by Wise Publications.

Compiled by Peter Evans and Peter Lavender.
Music processed by Peter Lavender.
Cover photograph courtesy of London Features International.

Your Guarantee of Quality:
As publishers, we strive to produce every book to the highest commercial standards.
This book has been carefully designed to minimise awkward page turns
and to make playing from it a real pleasure.
Throughout, the printing and binding have been planned to ensure a sturdy,
attractive publication which should give years of enjoyment.
If your copy fails to meet our high standards, please inform us and we will gladly replace it.

Music Sales' complete catalogue describes thousands of titles and is
available in full colour sections by subject, direct from Music Sales Limited.
Please state your areas of interest and send a cheque/postal order for £1.50 for postage to:
Music Sales Limited, Newmarket Road, Bury St. Edmunds, Suffolk IP33 3YB.

This publication is not authorised
for sale in the United States of America
and/or Canada.

Wise Publications
London/New York/Paris/Sydney/Copenhagen/Madrid

1
A Fine Romance

Music by Jerome Kern
Words by Dorothy Fields

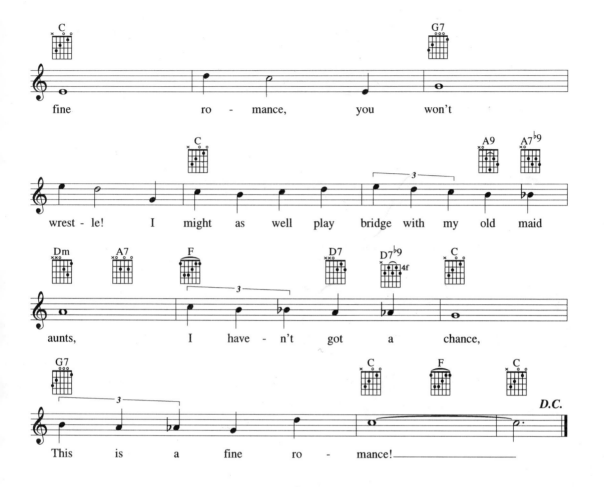

fine ro - mance, you won't wrest - le! I might as well play bridge with my old maid aunts, I have - n't got a chance, This is a fine ro - mance!

2. A fine romance with no kisses,
   A fine romance, my friend, this is!
   We two should be like clams in a dish of chowder,
   But we just fizz like parts of a Seidlitz powder!
   A fine romance with no clinches,
   A fine romance with no pinches!
   You're just as hard to land as the Ile de France,
   I haven't got a chance,
   This is a fine romance!

3. A fine romance, my dear Duchess,
   Two old fogies who need crutches!
   True love should have the thrills that a healthy crime has,
   We don't have half the thrill that the March Of Time has!
   A fine romance, my good woman,
   My strong "Aged In The Wood" woman!
   You never give the orchids I send a glance,
   No! You like cactus plants!
   This is a fine romance!

2
A Garden In The Rain

Words by James Dyrenforth
Music by Carroll Gibbons

3
All Of Me

Words & Music by Seymour Simons & Gerald Marks

Moderately

You took my kiss - es and you took my love,——

You taught me how to care. Am I to be—— just the

rem - nant of—— a one - sid - ed love—— af - fair?

All you took I glad - ly gave, There's noth - ing left for

me to save. All of me,—— Why not take

all of me?—— Can't you see—— I'm no good with - out you?——

4
All Or Nothing At All

Words & Music by Arthur Altman & Jack Lawrence

All_____ or noth - ing at all,_____
All_____ or noth - ing at all,_____

Half a love nev - er ap - pealed to me,_____
If it's love there is no in be - tween,_____

If your heart nev - er could
Why be - gin, then cry for some - thing that

yield to me,_____ Then I'd rath - er have
might have been,_____ No, I'd rath - er have

noth - ing at all.
noth - ing at

all._____

But please don't bring your lips so close to my

5
All The Things You Are

Music by Jerome Kern
Words by Oscar Hammerstein II

6
All The Way

Words by Sammy Cahn
Music by James Van Heusen

7
Among My Souvenirs

Words by Edgar Leslie
Music by Horatio Nicholls

8
Angel Eyes

Words by Earl Brent
Music by Matt Dennis

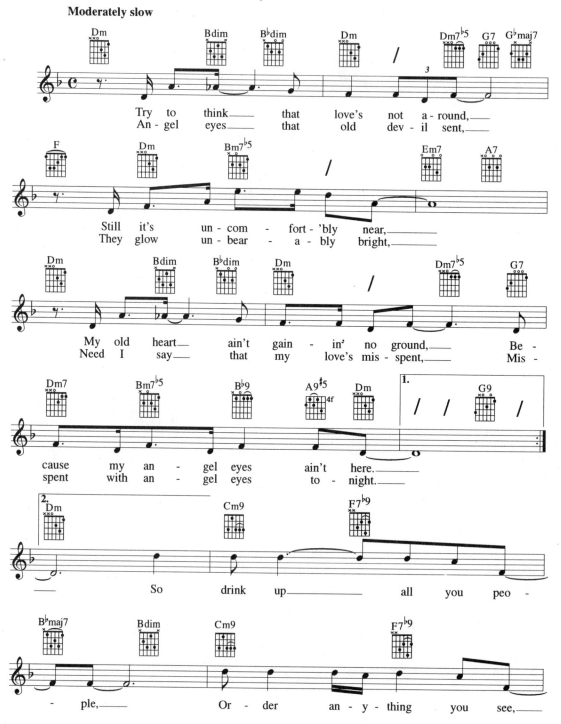

Moderately slow

Try to think that love's not a-round,
An - gel eyes that old dev - il sent,

Still it's un - com - fort - 'bly near,
They glow un - bear - a - bly bright,

My old heart ain't gain - in' no ground,
Need I say that my love's mis - spent,

cause my an - gel eyes ain't here.
spent with an - gel eyes to - night.

So drink up all you peo -

- ple, Or - der an - y - thing you see,

9
April Played The Fiddle

Words by Johnny Burke
Music by James Monaco

10
Because Of You

Words & Music by Arthur Hammerstein & Dudley Wilkinson

Moderately

All my days were lone - ly ones, Till you came a - long. Now my days are hap - py ones, You filled my life with song. Be - cause of you there's a song in my heart,_____ Be - cause of you my ro - mance had its start._____ Be - cause of you the sun will shine, The moon and

11
Begin The Beguine

Words & Music by Cole Porter

12
Bye Bye Baby

Words by Leo Robin
Music by Jule Styne

13
Brazil

Music by Ary Barroso
English Lyric by S. K. Russell

14
Christmas Dreaming

Words & Music by Irving Gordon & Lester Lee

15
Call Me Irresponsible

Words by Sammy Cahn
Music by Jimmy Van Heusen

Moderately slow

Call me ir - re - spon - si - ble,

Call me un - re - li - a - ble, Throw in

un - de - pend - a - ble too,

Do my fool - ish al - i - bis bore

you? Well, I'm not too clev - er, I

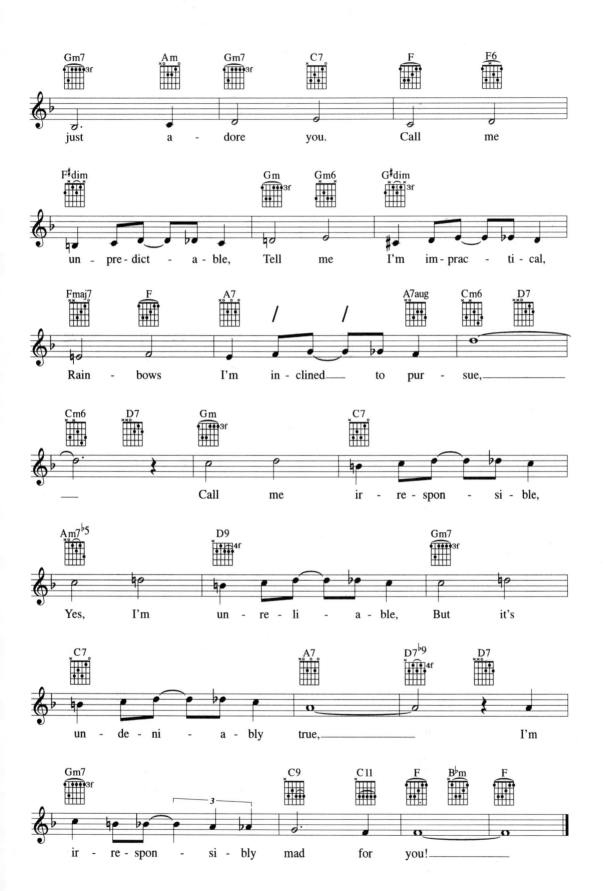

16
Come Dance With Me

Words & Music by Sammy Cahn & Jimmy Van Heusen

Hey there cutes! Put on your danc-ing boots and come dance with me, Come dance with me, What an eve-ning for some terp-si-chore! Pret-ty face, I know a swing-ing place, Come on, dance with me, Ro-mance with me on a crowd-ed floor. And while the rhy-thm pings, Oh what love-ly things I'll be

17
Come Fly With Me

Lyrics by Sammy Cahn
Music by James Van Heusen

18
Dear Heart

Words by Jay Livingston & Ray Evans
Music by Henry Mancini

19
Do I Worry?

Words & Music by Stanley Cowan & Bobby Worth

Per - haps you won - der how I feel a - bout your sud - den change. I thought at last that this was real, But since you're act - ing strange - ly: Do I

wor - ry 'cause you're step - pin' out? Do I
wor - ry when the ice - man calls? Do I

wor - ry 'cause you've got me in doubt?—— Tho' your
wor - ry if Ni - a - g'ra falls,———— Tho' you're

20
Day By Day

Words & Music by Sammy Cahn, Axel Stordahl & Paul Weston

21
Don't Blame Me

Words & Music by Jimmy McHugh & Dorothy Fields

22
Don't Worry 'Bout Me

Words by Ted Koehler
Music by Rube Bloom

23
East Of The Sun
(And West Of The Moon)

Moderately   Words & Music by Brooks Bowman

I wish that we could live up in the sky,_____ Where
we could find a place a-way up high,_____ To
live a-mong the stars, the sun, the moon, Just you and I.
East of the sun,_____ And west of the moon,_____
We'll build a dream-house_____ of
love dear, Near to the sun in the
day, Near to the moon at night, We'll

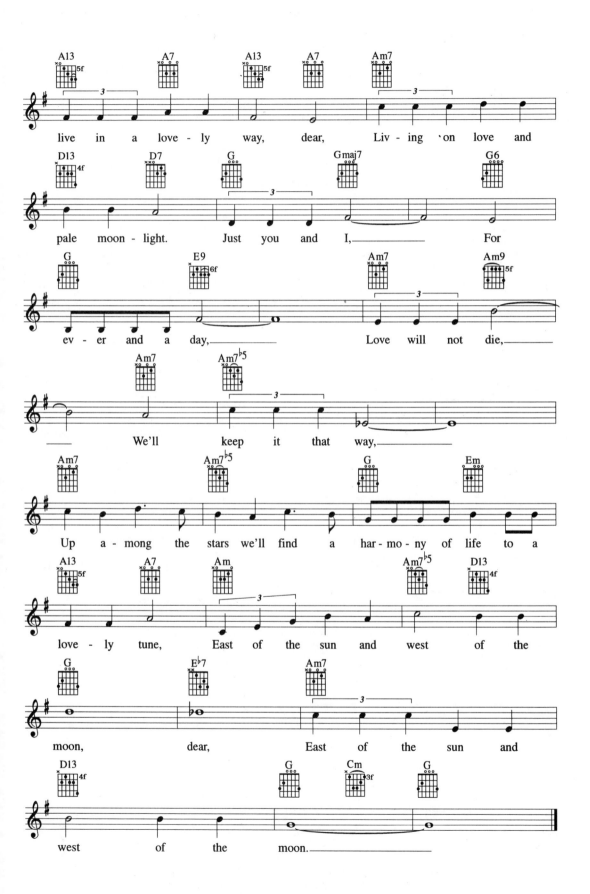

24
Everything Happens To Me

Words by Tom Adair
Music by Matt Dennis

25
Fly Me To The Moon
(In Other Words)

Words & Music by Bart Howard

Moderately slow

Po - ets of - ten use man - y words to say a sim - ple thing,_____ It takes thought and time and rhyme to make a po - em sing._____ With mu - sic and words I've been play - ing,_____ For you I have writ - ten a song,_____ To be sure that you'll know what I'm say - ing,_____ I'll trans - late as I go a - long:_____ Fly me to the moon and let me

26
Fools Rush In

Words by Johnny Mercer
Music by Rube Bloom

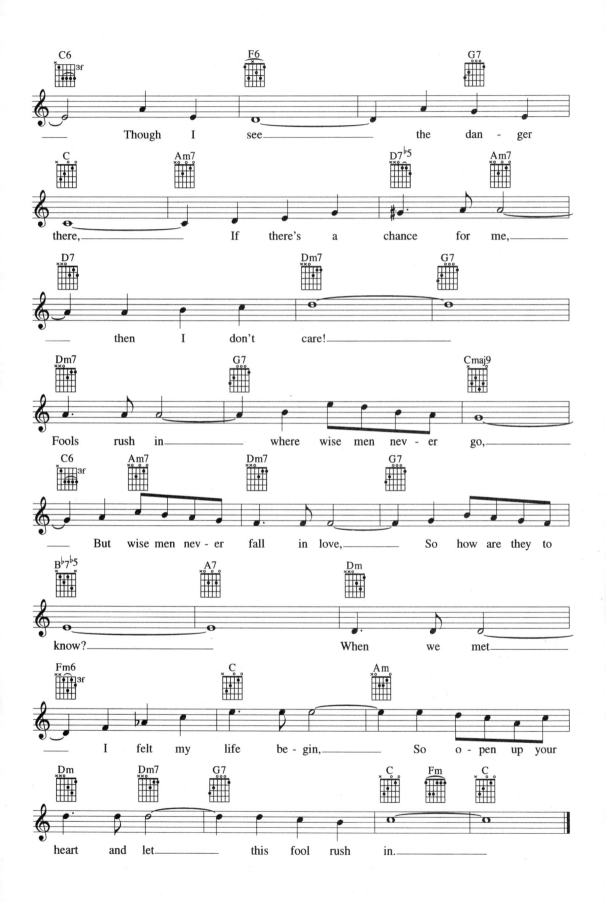

27
From Here To Eternity

Words by Robert Wells
Music by Fred Karger

28
Full Moon And Empty Arms

Music by Sergei Rachmaninov
Words & Arrangement by Buddy Kaye & Ted Mossman

29
Goodbye

Words & Music by Gordon Jenkins

30
Guys And Dolls

Words & Music by Frank Loesser

When you see a guy___ reach for
see a dame___ change for the

stars in the sky,___ You can bet that he's do-
shape of her frame,___ You can bet she's re-duc-

-ing it for some doll.___ When you spot a
-ing it for some guy.___ When you find a

John wait-ing out in the rain,___ Chan-ces
Doll with her dia-mond in hock,___ Rest as-

are he's in-sane as on-ly a John can
sured that the rock has gone to re-stock some

be for a Jane.___ When you meet a gent___
gen-tle-man Jock.___ When you see a mouse___

31
Granada

Music by Agustin Lara
English Lyric by Dorothy Dodd

Gra - na - da, —— I'm fall - ing un - der your spell, —— And if you could speak what a fas - cin - at - ing tale you would tell, —— Of an age —— the world has long for - got - ten, —— Of an age —— that weaves a si - lent mag - ic in Gra - na - da to - day! The

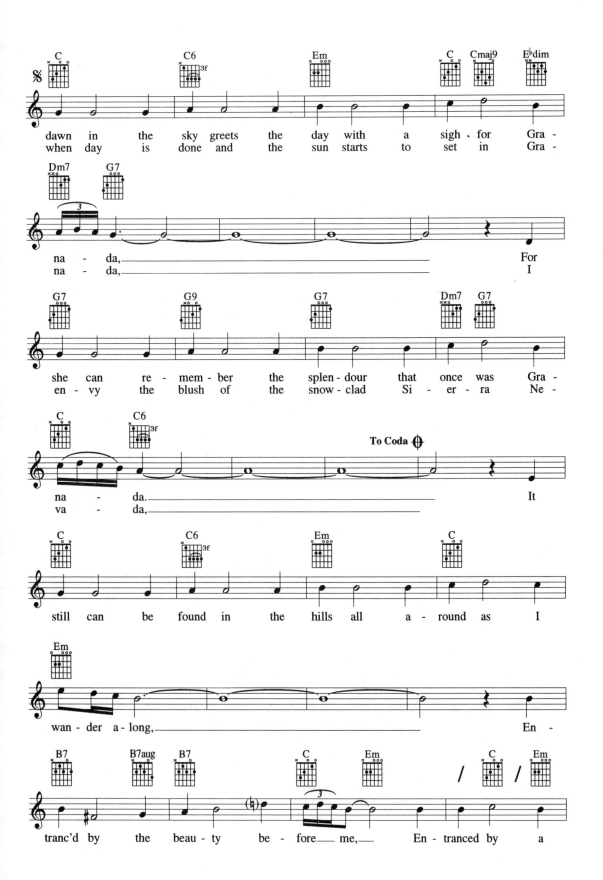

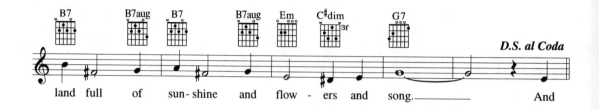

D.S. al Coda

land full of sun- shine and flow - ers and song._____ And

Coda

_____ For soon it will wel - come the

stars while a thou- sand gui - tars play a soft hab - an -

er - a,_____ Then moon - lit Gra - na - da will

live a- gain the glo - ry of yes- ter- day, Ro - man - tic and

gay!_____

32
Here's That Rainy Day

Words & Music by Johnny Burke & Jimmy Van Heusen

33
Have Yourself A
Merry Little Christmas

Words & Music by Hugh Martin & Ralph Blane

34
Hey Jealous Lover

Words & Music by Sammy Cahn, Kay Twomey & Bee Walker

Moderate (solid beat)

N.C.

(Instrumental)

Hey! Jeal - ous lov - er,_____ You're act - ing so

strange, Hey! Jeal - ous lov - er,_____

What is mak - ing you change?_____ Hey! Jeal - ous

lov - er,_____ How wrong can you be?

I'm yours, ev - er faith - ful,_____ Just be faith - ful to

35
High Hopes

Words by Sammy Cahn
Music by James Van Heusen

Moderately

Next time you're found— with your chin on the ground,— There's a
(See lyrics 2 & 3)

lot to be learned,— So look a - round.——

Just what makes that lit - tle ol' ant— think he'll move that

rub - ber tree plant,— An - y-one knows— an ant can't—

move a rub - ber tree plant. But he's got high—— hopes, He's got

high—— hopes, He's got high ap - ple pie in the

sky—— hopes, So an - y time you're get - tin' low,

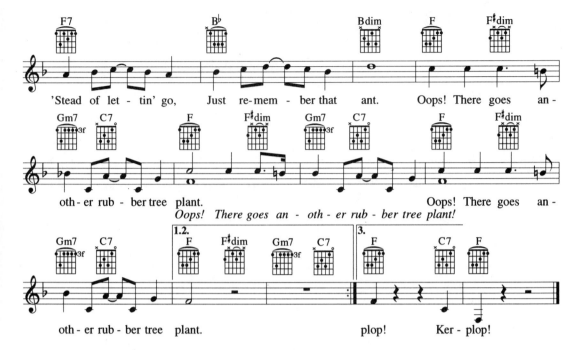

'Stead of let - tin' go, Just re-mem - ber that ant. Oops! There goes an -

oth - er rub - ber tree plant.   Oops! There goes an -
Oops! There goes an - oth - er rub - ber tree plant!

1.2. oth - er rub - ber tree plant.   **3.** plop!   Ker - plop!

2. When troubles call and your back's to the wall,
   There's a lot to be learned,
   That wall could fall.
   Once there was a silly ol' ram,
   Thought he'd punch a hole in a dam,
   No one could make that ram scram,
   He kept buttin' that dam.
   'Cause he had high hopes,
   He had high hopes,
   He had high apple pie in the sky hopes.
   So any time you're feelin' bad,
   'Stead of feelin' sad,
   Just remember that ram.
   Oops! There goes a billion kilowatt dam!
   Oops! There goes a billion kilowatt dam!
   Oops! There goes a billion kilowatt dam!

3. When troubles call and your back's to the wall,
   There's a lot to be learned,
   That wall could fall.
   Once there was a silly ol' ram,
   Thought he'd punch a hole in a dam,
   No one could make that ram scram,
   He kept buttin' that dam.
   So keep your high hopes,
   Keep your high hopes,
   Keep those high apple pie in the sky hopes.
   A problem's just a toy balloon,
   They'll be bursting soon,
   They're just bound to go "Pop!"
   Oops! There goes another problem, kerplop!
   Oops! There goes another problem, kerplop!
   Oops! There goes another problem, kerplop!
   Kerplop!

36
I Hear A Rhapsody

Words & Music by George Fragos, Jack Baker & Dick Gasparre

37
I Only Have Eyes For You

Words by Al Dubin
Music by Harry Warren

My love must be a kind of blind love,
I know the thrill of na-ture's won - ders,

I can't see an-y-one but you,
I know they're lurk-ing ev-'ry - where.

And, dear, I won-der if you find
I'm sure I'm mak-ing man-y blun -

love an op-ti-cal il-lu-sion too?
ders by pass-ing up those won-ders rare.

Are the stars out to-night, I don't know if it's cloud-y or

bright, 'Cause I on-ly have eyes for you,

38
I Think Of You

Words & Music by Jack Elliott & Don Marcotte

39
I Wanna Be Around

Words & Music by Johnny Mercer & Sadie Vimmerstedt

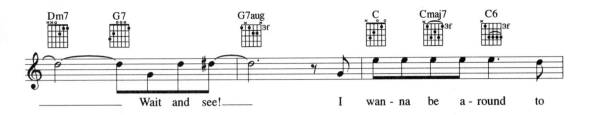

_____ Wait and see!_____ I wan - na be a - round to

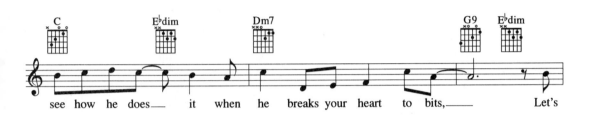

see how he does___ it when he breaks your heart to bits,_____ Let's

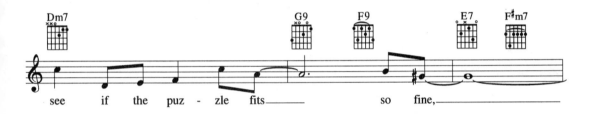

see if the puz – zle fits_____ so fine,_____

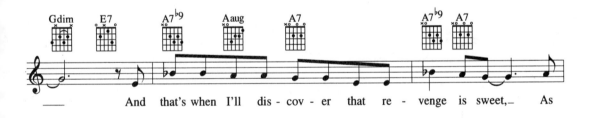

____ And that's when I'll dis - cov - er that re - venge is sweet,_ As

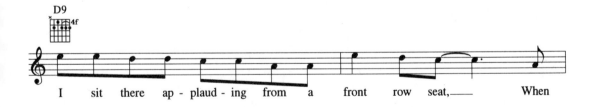

I sit there ap - plaud - ing from a front row seat,_____ When

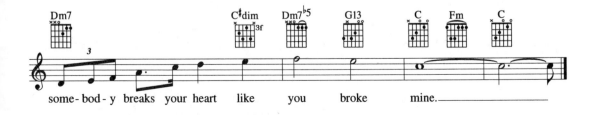

some-bod - y breaks your heart like you broke mine._____

40
I Wish You Love

Music & Original Lyrics by Charles Trenet
English Lyrics by Albert A. Beach

41
I'll Never Smile Again, Until I Smile At You

Words & Music by Ruth Lowe

42
I'll Remember April

Words & Music by Don Raye, Gene de Paul & Patricia Johnson

43
I'm Beginning To See
The Light

Words & Music by Harry James, Duke Ellington,
Johnny Hodges & Don George

44
I'm Gettin' Sentimental Over You

Words by Ned Washington
Music by Geo. Bassman

45
I'm Gonna Live Till I Die

Words & Music by Al Hoffman, Walter Kent & Mann Curtis

I'm gon - na live____ till I die,____
say____ "What a guy!"

I'm gon - na laugh____ 'stead of cry,____
I'm gon - na play____ for the sky,

I'm gon - na take the town____ and turn it
Ain't gon - na miss a thing;____ I'm gon - na

up - side down,____ } I'm gon - na live, live, live____ till I
have my fling,____ }

die. They're gon - na The blues - 'll lay low,____

____ I'll make 'em stay low,____ They'll nev - er trail ov -

46
I'm Gonna Make It All The Way

Words & Music by Floyd Huddleston

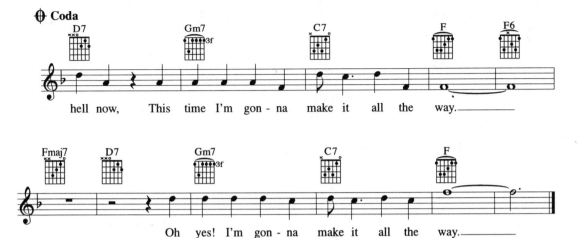

Coda

| D7 | Gm7 | C7 | F | F6 |

hell now,   This time I'm gon - na   make it   all the   way._____

| Fmaj7 | D7 | Gm7 | C7 | F |

Oh   yes! I'm gon - na   make it   all the   way._____

2. You hurt me and abused me,
   Took advantage of and used me,
   I swear it almost made a wreck of me.
   When I needed your devotion,
   You were never in the notion,
   You were colder than an iceberg in the sea.
   Love to you had lost its splendor,
   My pride went out the window
   When you left me I kept beggin' you to stay.
   But now my heart is healin',
   I've got a real good feelin',
   I think I'm gonna make it all the way.

3. My troubles came in bunches,
   I kept rollin' with the punches,
   You'd shoot me down, I'd get back up again.
   I tried to be your lover,
   In no time I discovered
   Your lovin' cup was not for me to win.
   Your kisses weren't the same
   But I kept tryin' to fan the flame,
   'Til I just couldn't face another day.
   You can't blame me for tryin',
   Now that I've stopped cryin',
   I think I'm gonna make it all the way.

4. I tried my best to fake it
   But a smilin' face don't make it,
   'Cause in my heart I knew there was no hope.
   Each place reminded me of
   The memories of your love,
   I'd come right to the end of my rope.
   That's when I met my new friend,
   She's just a passing-through friend,
   But she treats me like love is here to stay.
   It's workin' out real well now,
   And you can go to hell now,
   This time I'm gonna make it all the way.
   Oh yes! I'm gonna make it all the way.

47
I'm Gonna Sit Right Down And Write Myself A Letter

Words by Joe Young
Music by Fred E. Ahlert

48
I've Got You Under My Skin

Words & Music by Cole Porter

49
If You Are But A Dream

Words by Moe Jaffe & Jack Fulton
Music by Nat Bonx

50
In The Blue Of Evening

Words by Tom Adair
Music by D'Artega

Night draws a vel-ve-ty cur-tain o-ver the cares of the day. My heart is light, for it's cer-tain that I'll be meet-ing you in se-cret ren-dez-vous. In the blue of eve-ning, When you ap-pear close to me, dear one,— There in the dusk we'll share a dream——— rev-er-ie. In the blue of eve-ning, While crick-ets call

51
It Was A Very Good Year

Words & Music by Ervin Drake

Moderately slow

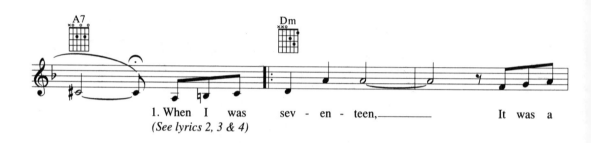

1. When I was sev - en - teen,___ It was a
(See lyrics 2, 3 & 4)

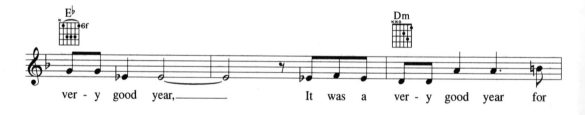

ver - y good year,___ It was a ver - y good year for

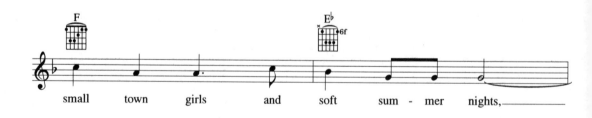

small town girls and soft sum - mer nights,___

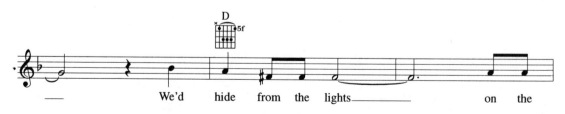

___ We'd hide from the lights___ on the

vil - lage green,_____ When I was sev - en - teen._____

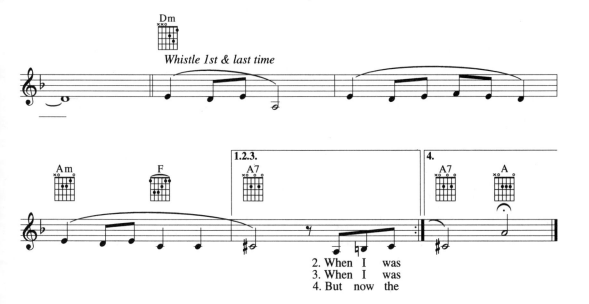

Whistle 1st & last time

2. When I was
3. When I was
4. But now the

2. When I was twenty-one,
   It was a very good year,
   It was a very good year for city girls
   Who lived up the stair,
   With perfumed hair
   That came undone,
   When I was twenty-one.

3. When I was thirty-five,
   It was a very good year,
   It was a very good year for blue blooded girls
   Of independent means,
   We'd ride in limousines,
   Their chauffeurs would drive,
   When I was thirty-five.

4. But now the days are short,
   I'm in the autumn of the year,
   And now I think of my life as vintage wine
   From fine old kegs,
   From the brim to the dregs,
   It poured sweet and clear,
   It was a very good year.

52
It's Nice To Go Trav'ling

Words by Sammy Cahn
Music by James Van Heusen

It's ver - y nice_____ to go trav - 'ling, but it's

oh so_____ nice_____ to come home. *(Instrumental)*

_____ to come home. No more cus - toms!

Repeat to fade

Burn the pass - port!   No more pack - ing!
And un - pack - ing!   Light the bon - fires!
Get my slip - pers!   Start a piz - za!

2. You will find the maedchen
   And the gay muchachas are rare,
   But they can't compare with the sexy line
   That parades each day at Sunset and Vine.
   It's quite the life to play gypsy
   And roam as gypsies will roam,
   It's quite the life to play gypsy
   But your heart starts singing
   When you're homeward singing 'cross the foam,
   And the Hudson river
   Makes you start to quiver
   Like the latest flivver
   That simply is dripping with chrome.

   It's very nice to go trav'ling,
   But it's oh so nice to come home!

53
I Could Have Told You

Words & Music by Carl Sigman & Arthur Williams

54
Lean Baby

Words by Roy Alfred
Music by Billy May

Medium bounce

My lean ba - by, tall____ and thin,____

Five - feet - sev - en of bones and skin,____ But when she

tells me may - be she____ loves me,____ I feel as

mel - low as a fel - low can be.____

She's so skin - ny, she's____ so drawn,____ When

she stands side - ways you think she's gone,____ But when she

calls me ba - by, I____ feel fine____ to think she's

*add. male lyric

fran - tic - 'lly ro - man - tic - 'lly mine._____ She's

slen - der,_____ but she's ten - der,_____ She_____
chased her_____ and I caught her,_____ Then a

makes my heart sur - ren - der,_____ And ev - 'ry night_____ when
dia - mond ring I bought her,_____ The dia - monds shine,_____ the

I hold her tight,_____ The feel - ing is nice,_____ my arms can
ring is so fine,_____ But here is the twist,_____ she wears it

go a - round_____ twice! My lean ba - by, she's_____
right on her_____ wrist!

_____ so slim,_____ A broom - stick's wid - er but

not as trim,_____ And when she starts to kiss me, Then_____

_____ I know_____ I love her so, I'll nev - er ev - er let her go.

55
Learnin' The Blues

Words & Music by Dolores Vicki Silvers

56
Let's Get Away From It All

Music by Matt Dennis
Words by Tom Adair

57
Love And Marriage

Words by Sammy Cahn
Music by James Van Heusen

Love and mar - riage, love and mar - riage,

1. Go to - geth - er · like a horse and car - riage,
2. It's an in - sti - tute you can't dis - par - age,

This I tell ya broth - er, ya
Ask the lo - cal gen - try, and

can't have one with - out the oth - er.
they will say it's el - e -

men - t'ry. Try, try, try to sep - ar - ate them,

It's an il - lu - sion. Try, try,

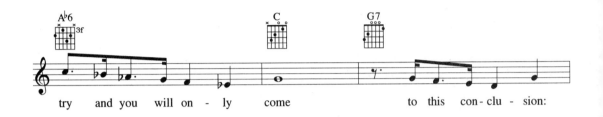

try and you will on - ly come to this con - clu - sion:

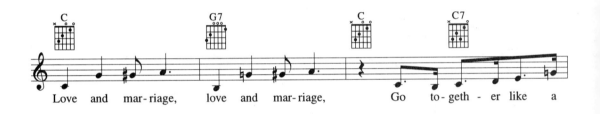

Love and mar- riage, love and mar- riage, Go to- geth - er like a

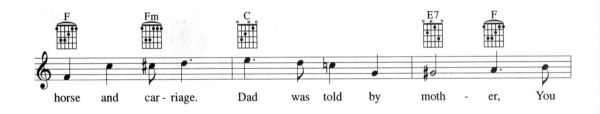

horse and car - riage. Dad was told by moth - er, You

can't have one, you can't have none, You can't have one with- out the

oth - er!

58
Love's Been Good To Me

Words & Music by Rod McKuen

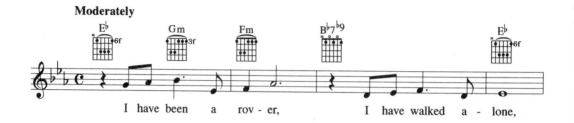

I have been a rov - er, I have walked a - lone,

Hiked a hun - dred high - ways, Nev - er found a home.

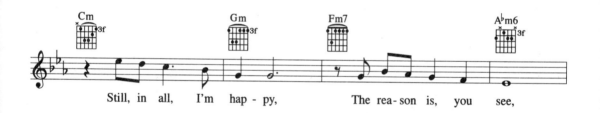

Still, in all, I'm hap - py, The rea - son is, you see,

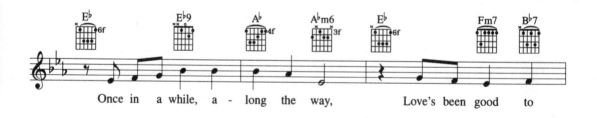

Once in a while, a - long the way, Love's been good to

me. { There was a girl in Den - ver,
    { There was a girl in Port - land,

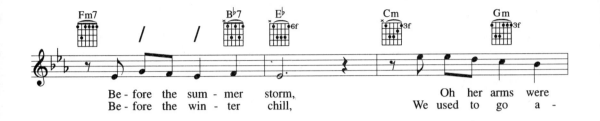

Be - fore the sum - mer storm, Oh her arms were
Be - fore the win - ter chill, We used to go a -

ten - der! Oh her arms were warm! And she could
court - ing a - long Oct - o - ber Hill, And she could

smile a - way the thun - der, Kiss a - way the
laugh a - way the dark clouds, Cry a - way the

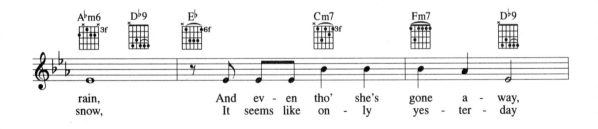

rain, And ev - en tho' she's gone a - way,
snow, It seems like on - ly yes - ter - day

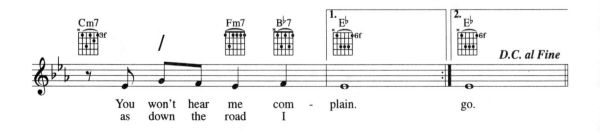

You won't hear me com - plain. go.
as down the road I

59
Luck Be A Lady

Words & Music by Frank Loesser

They call you Lad-y Luck but there is room for doubt, At times you have a ver-y un-lad-y-like way of run-ning out.— You're on a date with me, The pick-ings have been lush, And yet be-fore this eve-ning is ov-er you might give me the brush.— You might for-get your man-ners, You might re-fuse to stay, And so the best that I can do is pray!— Luck be a lad-y to-night,———

60
Lover

Music by Richard Rodgers
Words by Lorenz Hart

61
Moon River

Music by Henry Mancini
Words by Johnny Mercer

62
Moonlight On The Ganges

Words by Chester Wallace
Music by Sherman Myers

1. Dew - drops glis - ten - ing, no one lis - ten - ing, By the Gan - ges
2. In a car - a - van far from Hin - du - stan slow - ly jogs a

some - one whis - per - ing to a love - ly maid,_____
wea - ry cam - el man 'neath the har - vest moon._____

"Tho' to - mor - row, dear, you will yearn, Don't you sor - row, dear,
Fields of cot - ton he used to stray, Not for - got - ten but

I'll re - turn to my pret - ty maid."_____
far a - way, He'll be near - ing soon._____

63
Moonlight Becomes You

Music by Jimmy Van Heusen
Words by Johnny Burke

64
More Than You Know

Words & Music by William Rose & Edward Eliscu
Music by Vincent Youmans

65
Mrs Robinson

Words & Music by Paul Simon

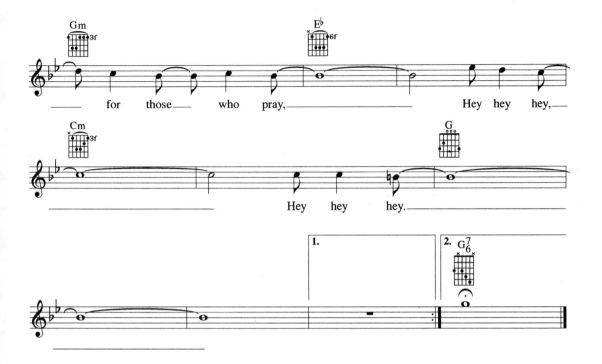

for those— who pray,————— Hey hey hey,—

Hey hey hey.————

1.

2. G$^7_6$

3. Sitting on a sofa on a Sunday afternoon,
   Going to the candidate's debate.
   Laugh about it, shout about it,
   When you've got to choose,
   Every way you look at it, you lose.
   Where have you gone, Joe Dimaggio?
   A nation turns its lonely eyes to you,
   Woo woo woo.
   What's that you say, Mrs. Robinson?
   "Joltin' Joe" has left and gone away,
   Hey hey hey,
   Hey hey hey.

66
My Kind Of Girl

Words & Music by Leslie Bricusse

Moderate swing

She walks like an an - gel walks,
wise like an an - gel's wise,

She talks like an an - gel talks,
With eyes like an an - gel's eyes,

And her hair has a kind of curl,
And a smile like a kind of pearl,

To my mind she's my kind of girl.
To my mind she's my kind of girl.

— She's — Pret - ty lit - tle face, That face just

knocks me off my feet. Pret - ty lit - tle feet, She's real - ly

sweet e - nough to eat!____ She looks like an an - gel

looks, She e - ven cooks like an an - gel

cooks, And my mind's in a kind of

whirl, Be - cause to my mind she's my kind____ of

girl._____ She girl. And my

heart's kind - a full of joy, Be - cause she's

told me____ I'm her kind____ of boy.____

67
My Kind Of Town (Chicago Is)

Words by Sammy Cahn
Music by Jimmy Van Heusen

Any city name of three syllables can replace Chicago, i.e., Manhattan, Las Vegas, etc.

68
New York, New York

Words by Fred Ebb
Music by John Kander

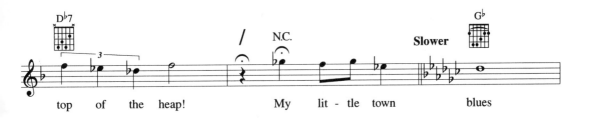

top of the heap! My lit - tle town blues

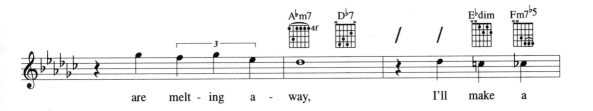

are melt - ing a - way, I'll make a

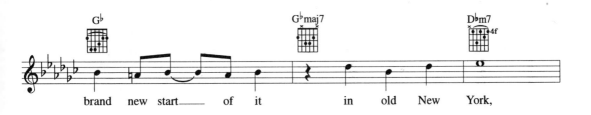

brand new start___ of it in old New York,

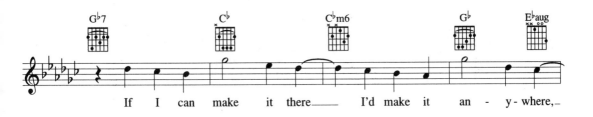

If I can make it there___ I'd make it an - y - where,___

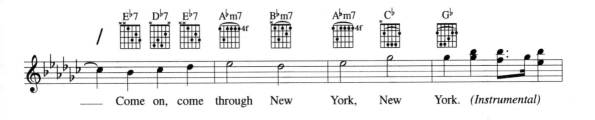

___ Come on, come through New York, New York. *(Instrumental)*

69
Oh Look At Me Now

Words by John DeVries
Music by Joe Bushkin

Moderate easy swing

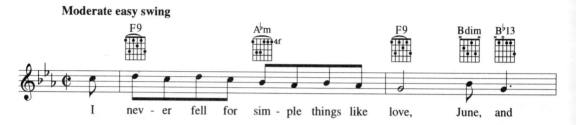

I nev - er fell for sim - ple things like love, June, and

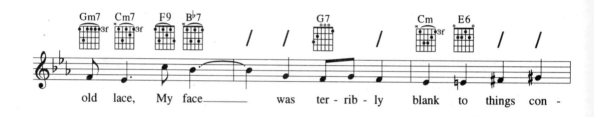

old lace, My face_____ was ter - rib - ly blank to things con -

cern - ing L'a - mour,_____ I'm real - ly read - y now for sure, For

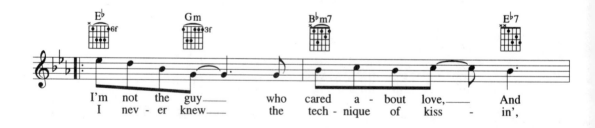

I'm not the guy_____ who cared a - bout love,_____ And
I nev - er knew_____ the tech - nique of kiss - in',

I'm not the guy_____ who cared a - bout for - tunes and such,_____
I nev - er knew_____ the thrill I could get_____ from your touch,_____

70
On The Sunny Side Of The Street

Words by Dorothy Fields
Music by Jimmy McHugh

71
One For My Baby
(And One More For The Road)

Words by Johnny Mercer
Music by Harold Arlen

Slow blues tempo

72
September Song

Words by Maxwell Anderson
Music by Kurt Weill

73
Somethin' Stupid

Words & Music by C. Carson Parks

Moderately

I know I stand in line___ un - til you
prac - tice ev - 'ry day to find___ some

think you have the time to spend an eve - nin' with me,___
cle - ver lines to say to make the mean - ing come through,___

And if we go some place to dance, I
But then I think I'll wait un - til the

know that there's a chance you won't be leav - in' with me,___
eve - nin' gets___ late and I'm a - lone___ with you,___

Then af - ter - wards we drop in - to a
The time is right, your per - fume fills my

74
Stella By Starlight

Music by Victor Young
Words by Ned Washington

75
Stormy Weather

Words by Ted Koehler
Music by Harold Arlen

76
Strangers In The Night

Words by Charles Singleton & Eddie Snyder
Music by Bert Kaempfert

77
Nice 'N' Easy

Words by Marilyn & Alan Bergman
Music by Lew Spence

78
Thanks For The Memory

Words & Music by Leo Robin & Ralph Rainger

79
Tangerine

Music by Victor Schertzinger
Words by Johnny Mercer

South A - mer - i - can stor - ies____ tell of a girl who's quite a dream,____ The beau - ty of her race.

Though you doubt all the stor - ies,____ And think the tales are just a bit ex - treme,____ Wait till you see her face!____ Tan - ger - ine,____ She is all they claim,____ With her eyes of night and lips as bright as

80
Teach Me Tonight

Music by Gene De Paul
Lyrics by Sammy Cahn

81
The Christmas Waltz

Words by Sammy Cahn
Music by Jule Styne

Moderately

Frost - ed win - dow panes, _____ Can - dles gleam - ing in - side, Paint - ed can - dy canes _____ on the tree; San - ta's on his way, He's filled his sleigh with things, _____ Things for you and for me. It's that time of year, _____ When the

82
The Coffee Song

Words & Music by Bob Hilliard & Dick Miles

1. Way down a - mong Bra - zil - ians cof - fee
(2) date a girl and find out lat - er

beans grow by the bil - lions, So they've got to find those
she smells like a per - co - lat - or, Her per - fume was

ex - tra cups to fill, _____ They've got an
made right on to the grill, _____ Why, they could

aw - ful lot of cof - fee in Bra - zil. _____ You
per - co - late the o - cean in Bra - zil. _____ And

can't get cher - ry sod - a 'cause they've got to sell their
when their ham and eggs need sav - our, Cof - fee ketch - up

quo - ta and the way things are I guess they nev - er will, _____
gives them flav - our, Cof - fee pick - les way out - sell the dill, _____

—— They've got a zil - lion tons of cof - fee in Bra -
—— Why they put cof - fee in the cof - fee in Bra -

83
The Lady Is A Tramp

Words by Lorenz Hart
Music by Richard Rodgers

84
The Nearness Of You

Music by Hoagy Carmichael
Words by Ned Washington

85
The Night We Called It A Day

Words by Tom Adair
Music by Matt Dennis

(Instrumental) Au-thors and po-ets, in prose and in rhyme,

Seem to a-gree that night is the time of lov-ers' meet-ings,

Ro-man-tic greet-ings. To my mis-for-tune I found this a lie,

For it was night when you whis-pered "Good-bye," A night of mad-ness

that turned to sad-ness much too soon.———— There was a

moon out in space, But a cloud drift-ed ov-er it's
song of the spheres, Like a min-or la-ment in my

86
The Song Is You

Music by Jerome Kern
Words by Oscar Hammerstein II

87
(Love Is) The Tender Trap

Words by Sammy Cahn
Music by James Van Heusen

88
The Things We Did Last Summer

Words & Music by Sammy Cahn & Jule Styne

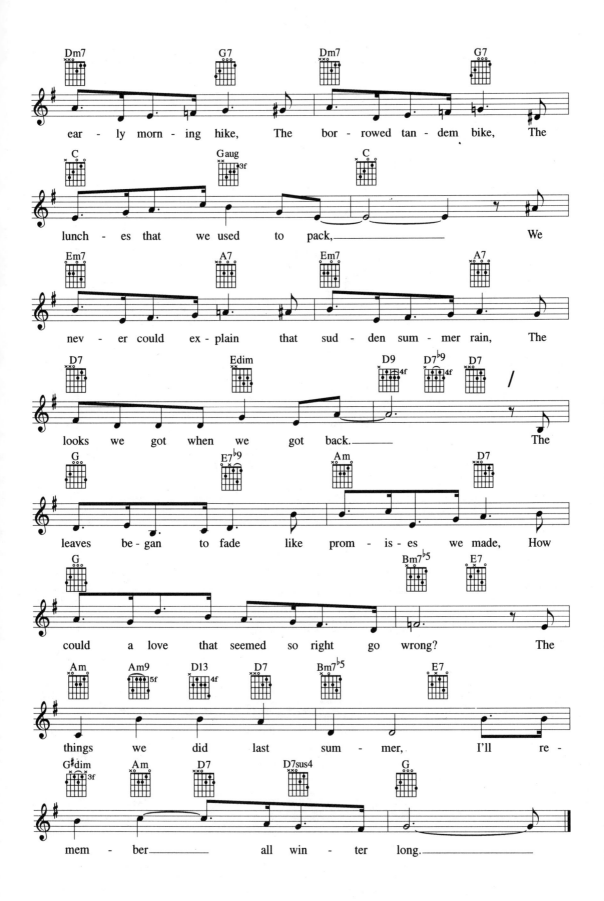

89
The Very Thought Of You

Words & Music by Ray Noble

90
That Old Black Magic

Music by Harold Arlen
Words by Johnny Mercer

Moderately

That old black mag - ic has me in it's spell,

That old black mag - ic that you weave so well,

Those i - cy fin - gers up and down my spine,

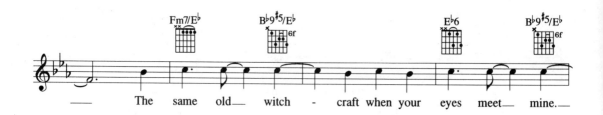

The same old witch - craft when your eyes meet mine.

The same old tin - gle that I feel in - side,

91
These Foolish Things

Words by Eric Maschwitz
Music by Jack Strachey

Moderately slow

E♭6 · · · · · · D♭9

Oh! Will you nev - er let me be?

E♭6 · · Cm · F13 · B♭9♭5 · B♭7

Oh! Will you nev - er set me free? The ties that bound us

E♭13 · G9♭5 · G7 · D♭13 · G♭7

are still a - round us, There's no es - cape that I can

F13 · F7 · Fm7♭5 · B♭7 · B♭m7 · E♭7 · A♭maj9

see. And still those lit - tle things re - main,

Cm7 · F7sus4 · F9 · B♭13 · B♭7aug · B♭9 · B♭aug

That bring me hap - pi - ness or pain:

E♭ · Cm7 · Fm9 · B♭7

A cig - a - rette that bears a lip - stick's tra - ces,
(See lyrics 2 & 3)

E♭ · Cm7 · F9 · B♭7

An air - line tick - et to ro - man - tic pla - ces,

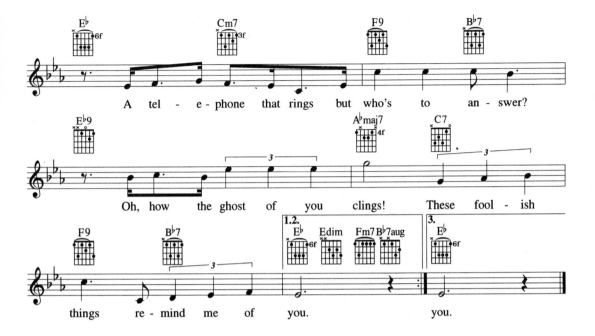

A tel - e - phone that rings but who's to an - swer?

Oh, how the ghost of you clings! These fool - ish

things re - mind me of you. you.

2. First daffodils and long excited cables,
And candle lights on little corner tables,
And still my heart has wings,
These foolish things remind me of you.
The park at evening when the bell has sounded,
The "Ile de France" with all the gulls around it,
The beauty that is Spring's,
These foolish things remind me of you.
How strange, how sweet, to find you still,
These things are dear to me,
They seem to bring you near to me.
The sigh of midnight trains in empty stations,
Silk stockings thrown aside, dance invitations,
Oh, how the ghost of you clings!
These foolish things remind me of you.

3. Gardenia perfume lingering on a pillow,
Wild strawberries only seven francs a kilo,
And still my heart has wings,
These foolish things remind me of you.
The smile of Garbo and the scent of roses,
The waiters whistling as the last bar closes,
The songs that Crosby sings,
These foolish things remind me of you.
How strange, how sweet, to find you still,
These things are dear to me,
They seem to bring you near to me.
The scent of smouldering leaves, the wail of steamers,
Two lovers on the street who walk like dreamers,
Oh, how the ghost of you clings!
These foolish things remind me of you.

92
Watch What Happens

Words by Norman Gimbel
Music by Michel Legrand

93
We'll Be Together Again

Words by Frankie Laine
Music by Carl Fischer

94
Witchcraft

Words by Carolyn Leigh
Music by Cy Coleman

95
Without A Song

Words by William Rose & Edward Eliscu
Music by Vincent Youmans

96
Wives And Lovers

Words by Hal David
Music by Burt Bacharach

Moderate jazz waltz

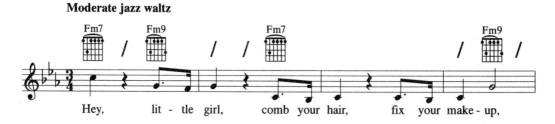

Hey,   lit - tle girl,   comb your hair,   fix your make - up,

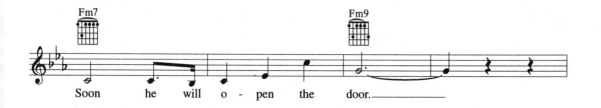

Soon   he will o - pen   the door.

Don't   think be - cause   there's a ring   on your fin - ger,

you   need - n't try an - y   more.   For

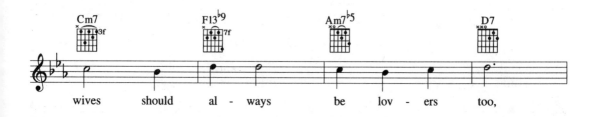

wives   should al - ways   be lov - ers   too,

97
Yesterdays

Music by Jerome Kern
Words by Otto Harbach

98
Yes Indeed (A Jive Spiritual)

Words & Music by Sy Oliver

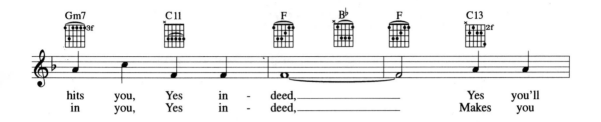

hits you, Yes in - deed,_____ Yes you'll
in you, Yes in - deed,_____ Makes you

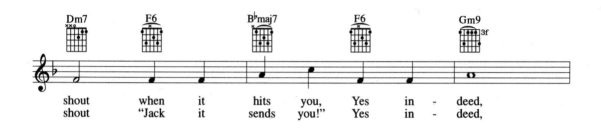

shout when it hits you, Yes in - deed,
shout "Jack it sends you!" Yes in - deed,

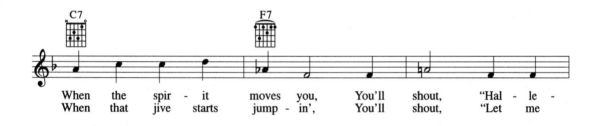

When the spir - it moves you, You'll shout, "Hal - le -
When that jive starts jump - in', You'll shout, "Let me

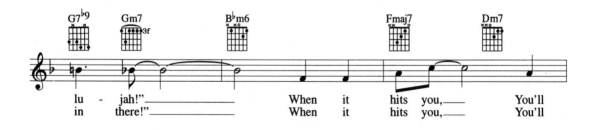

lu - jah!"_____ When it hits you,____ You'll
in there!"_____ When it hits you,____ You'll

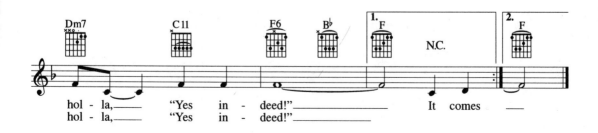

hol - la,____ "Yes in - deed!"_____ It comes ___
hol - la,____ "Yes in - deed!"_____

99
Yesterday

Words & Music by John Lennon & Paul McCartney

Moderately

Yes - ter - day,_____ All my trou - bles seemed so far a - way, Now it looks as though___ they're here to stay,_____ Oh, I be - lieve_____ in yes - ter - day._____ Sud - den - ly,_____ I'm not half the man___ I used to be, There's a shad - ow hang - ing ov - er me,_____ Oh, yes - ter - day_____ came sud - den - ly._____

100
You're Nobody 'Til Somebody Loves You

Words & Music by Russ Morgan, Larry Stock & James Cavanaugh

Moderately slow

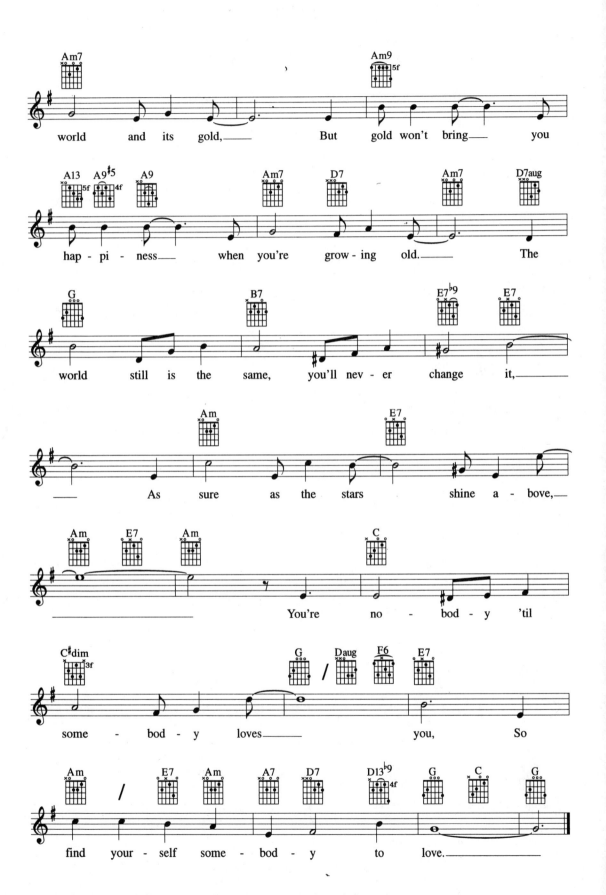

101
You, My Love

Words & Music by Mack Gordon & Jimmy Van Heusen